AF419702

Seeking Harmony

A book of poetry and prose

Danyelle Latrese

Copyright © 2022 by Danyelle Latrese

All rights reserved. No part of this book may be reproduced in any manner whatsoever without written permission except in the case of brief quotations embodied in critical articles and reviews.

First Printing, 2022

DEDICATION

To my fellow survivors of depression, anxiety, and any
form of trauma:

Vulnerability for us is no easy feat.
I hope that my willingness to bear it all assists you in your
quest to find some sort of harmony.

TRIGGER WARNING

suicide
depression
alcohol
substance abuse
sexual assault
death
body image
and potentially more.

If any of these triggers affect you, please practice self-care
before, after, and even during your reading.

CONTENTS

Unbroken

ACKNOWLEDGMENTS

Thank you to my friends and family that have stayed by my side and uplifted me throughout my wild ride in life. No matter how often we talk or see one another, please know that I love you dearly.

Thank you to my therapists for saving my life and helping me find reasons to smile again.

Thank you to anyone who has made me feel any form of love and happiness.

Thank you to the artists that created the illustrations included in this book.

Most importantly, thank you to 15-year-old Danyelle for discovering and diving into poetry for therapeutic reasons (before I even knew that I needed a therapist). I know that this is something that you've always wanted, so I hope I'm making you proud.

INTRODUCTION

They say a picture's worth a thousand words
Flying free in the sky filled with birds
Floating aimlessly above the ground
Hoping and praying not to be found
Because if they discover the truth,
They will then have the proof.
The puzzle piece that I've been missing
That I thought I could find through meaningless kissing
They'll learn how to shoot me off of this cloud
I'll be falling while they're standing proud
Well, at least they hope so,
Because what they don't know,
Is that I'm no longer afraid
No more do I feel like a meaningless blade
I've escaped the treacherous grass
Trying my best to bounce out with class
So this picture you see,
Is that of the real me.
Living no more lies
No more nights filled with cries
It may take some time,
But I'm ready to climb
The ladder leading to my dreams
To you, this picture may be just what it seems.
But for me, it's just the beginning of how to tell
The story of a girl named

Danyelle

LOST SOUL

She Screams.
she tries to talk,
but no one will listen.
the people she once trusted are gone,
nowhere to be found.
they tell her they love her
but end up leaving her
so she puts up a wall
not daring to let anyone enter.

She Screams.
she is tired of feeling hurt and unhappy.
she feels that she is alone in this huge world
with no one there to comfort her.
she wants to be loved,
but she can't find her way.

She Screams.
but no sound comes out.
no one can hear her.
no one knows how bad she feels.

She Screams.
there is still no noise
tears run from her eyes
but she can't control them.
there is nothing she can do.

She Screams
but when she sees that no one cares,
she breaks down.
she doesn't know what to do.
so she cries and cries
until there are no more tears in her eyes
to be released into the hard reality
and evil world.

The Thing

She's running as fast and as hard as possible,
trying to escape the evil thing behind her.
She looks back but doesn't see anything, yet,
she knows something is there, she can feel it.
She looks forward again trying to focus on getting away
but she doesn't see anywhere else to go.
She is in the middle of nowhere surrounded by trees
and the darkness of the night.
She tries to hide, but it sees her.
It walks up to her, squeezing her whole body.
Such an intense squeeze, it leaves her breathless.
She tries to scream for help,
but no noise comes from her mouth.
She can't escape it.
It keeps squeezing her and taking her breath
until her body is too weak.
She falls to the ground.
The thing is all over her trying to take her soul
and keep it for its own.
She wants so badly to get up
and for things to go back to the way they were.
How did things go from being perfect,
to how they are now?
She opens her eyes and she can see that the thing
has a familiar face.
She stares into its eyes and sees a whole world of pain.
She looks closer and realizes
that she is looking at herself.
She isn't in the middle of nowhere but her bedroom.
She stares at herself in the mirror
but doesn't think it is the real her.
It seems she is looking at a completely different person
who looks exactly like her.
"Who are you?" She asks the girl in the mirror,
but there is no response.
She stares into her own eyes,
wondering who and what she has become.

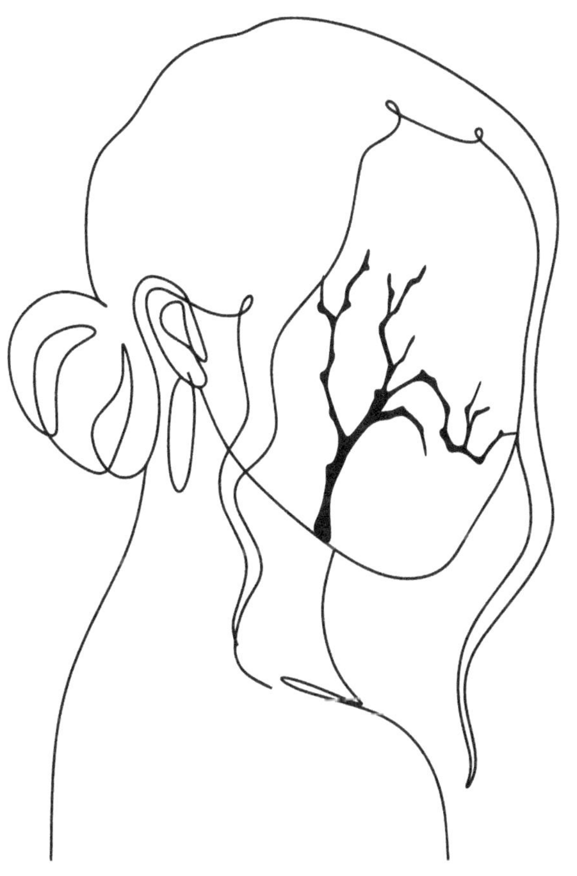

As I stare into this blank space
Everything in me disappears.
My face is plastered with an emotionless expression
As sound travels past my ears
Blinking fails to come naturally
My body goes numb
All I can do is sit here and think
But unfortunately, my mind has no thoughts.

My eyes start to glaze
It's only been a few minutes
But it feels more like days.

Once I'm caught within this trance,
I become unsure of how to escape.
I feel nothing and everything all at once.

I sit alone as the world goes silent
I lose myself in the moment
I forget who I am.
Who I once was.
Who I want to be.

I live within my head,
I am no longer a living, breathing person
I am nothing but a soul lost
In a place it doesn't understand.
I am trying to escape my body
Escape my mind
But the more I get lost
The more I lose that chance.

It's like an out-of-body experience.
I am within the body of someone that I don't know
Someone that I don't recognize
When I see my reflection
I look at my hands and I wonder how they are mine
I try to remember things from the past,

But it doesn't help.
I am not who they say I am.
I am not who I thought I was.
I have lost track of my former happiness.
I am lost.
I am stuck.
I am alone.

I Am Numb.

All I Have

Although others are surrounding me,
Although I communicate often,
Although others have felt the same,
I am alone.

All I have are my thoughts,
A mind full of words
That can't be unleashed.

A heart transmitting signals
Of what it wants to feel.

A wandering eye seeking visions
Of where my mind wants to be.

And although my mind should be here in the now,
It's wandering to a place far away.
A place that my heart has talked it into going,
A place my eyes can't wait to be.

All I have are my thoughts
And all they have is me.

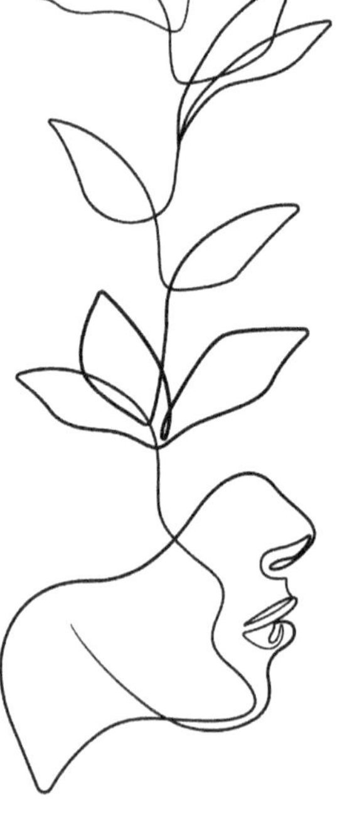

Construct

Time, in my opinion, is a construct
Another measure in which people try to control you
Everything, supposedly, revolves around time.

You're born and have all of these rules
Suddenly placed in front of you
All of these expectations and obligations
You're supposed to fulfill certain roles
And then…

Well then, it's too late.

You can no longer do anything.

Did you enjoy it?
Living by the expectations of others?
Letting them tell you what to do?
When to do it?
Were you really happy?
Did you only do it for them?
Did they pressure you into it?
Tell you that it's "necessary"?
That everyone has to do it at some point?
Was it all worth it?

I don't think it was.

I'm Not Okay,
  I never will be again.
  I don't know why I thought things would get better
  Why I thought they could turn around
  But they won't.
  I've gone through too much
  I've been broken too many times
  I've thought of death
  More times than I can even remember.

I'm Not Okay,
  I never will be again.
  I've spent too much of my life being unhappy,
  I can't just have a great life now
  No matter how much things seem to change
  Something always finds a way to ruin everything,
  Ruin me and all I've worked for.

I'm Not Okay,
  I never will be again.
  I've let go of everything I once believed in
  I've distanced myself from valuable people
  I've let the wrong ones come into my life
  In a way that they should have never come
  I thought I was happy and confident
  But my actions show that I'm more insecure than ever.

I'm Not Okay,
  I never will be again.
  I'm losing family members left and right
  Ones that I was never really close to
  Ones that I had many opportunities
  To spend time with
  I'm living a life that I don't agree with
  But I don't know how to stop it
  I don't know how to go back
  To the morals I once had.

I'm Not Okay,
I never will be again.
I'm releasing my body so easily
They tell me what I want to hear
They touch me in ways
That give me mixed feelings
I let them into my sacred self
The self that shouldn't be explored by man
I regret it later. I always do.
So why do I keep allowing it to happen?

I'm Not Okay,
I never will be again.
I don't know what to do with my life
I'm letting important things pass me by
I'm living carelessly
I simply don't care
When I know that I should
My entire personality has changed
I don't know who I am or where I'm going
I don't know what to do.

I'm Not Okay,
I never will be again.
My depression is increasing
Even though I try to hide it
I'm not happy and I know it
But I don't want to showcase it
I don't want people to see how weak I am
But I don't know if I can be strong anymore
I don't know how long it'll last
I just want it all to go away.

I'm Not Okay
I never will be again.
But in reality,
I never was okay
And that's the way
I'll always live.

Do You Know What Really Sucks About Depression?

It's the shame.
I spend every day of my life trying.
Trying not to let anyone in on my secret
Trying to appear as normal as possible
Trying to show the world that I'm happy.
But what does that even mean?
To be happy?

Am I supposed to smile constantly?
So long that my cheeks hurt?
So hard that it looks fake?
Because that's exactly what it is.
But apparently, that's okay.

A frown represents that something is wrong
"It will be okay"
"Everything will be all right"
I know but…no.
No, it won't
If everything was okay,
Would I be where I am now?
And where am I exactly?

At first, I thought that I was on cloud 9,
Floating high above all worry
But now?
Now I've fallen,
I've fallen 6ft deep and the worst part?
I didn't even land on my feet.

But how?
How did I get here?
How did things get this bad?
How could I allow all the hurt, the pain, the trauma
To make me sink this deep?

I'm so low with no hope
My ankle is tied to the anchor
Sinking so quickly that no one will find me
But I wonder,
Would they even look for me?
"I'll be here for you," they said
But as I look around, I see no one
Nothing but the depths of this ocean.

I have a million thoughts racing through my mind.
Question after question.
Answer after answer.
But there is one that stands out:

Do you know what really sucks about depression?
It's having this title,
This description,
This diagnosis,
This illness,
That doesn't allow me to know who I truly am.

Coping

Is a difficult thing to do.
You can think that you have everything figured out,
That things are finally good.
But it only takes one moment,
One feeling,
One memory,
To send you right back
Down the path of destruction.

So now you sit
And you think about all the chaos
All the hurt,
And you try to figure out how to numb it all,
How to pretend that everything's fine
So you seek alternative ways
All of which are unhealthy,

But who has the time to think about health
When your mind has been invaded
By such horrible thoughts?

The bouts of my anxiety start to creep in
I'm nervous,
I'm afraid,
I'm sweating,
Way too many thoughts are rushing through my mind
It's impossible to keep up with them
Like a high-speed chase, they're on a mission
But instead of finding an escape route
They've found a way to become ingrained in me
They've twisted themselves with my DNA,
We're one now.

I try my best to fight them off
To focus on things around me
The things I can touch
That I can see
That I can hear.
But all I can touch is my fidgeting body
All I can see are spots throughout the room
All I hear are negative things about myself
They're winning the race.

They've reached an area of my body where
It becomes impossible for me to resist
They have invaded my heart
It starts to beat faster and faster
I can hear it.
Its as if I'm laying on someone's chest
And listening to their heartbeat,
But this one is mine.

My body starts to heat up
I can feel my skin turning red
I can hear my voice begin to shake
My eyes can't focus
My hands try to move to distract me
I can't sit still
I'm shaking uncontrollably,

And then I hear a voice,
A tiny whisper that tells me to BREATHE.

I inhale and let it all out.
I repeat this a few more times
Until I can feel the release.
My body eases up,
The chase comes to a halt
Not because they have been captured
But because I've released them
From my body completely.

I regain my sense of awareness
I'm no longer lost
I'm no longer petrified
I'm where I need to be
And I have control of the situation,

I just need to

Breathe.

Empty

I can feel it all as it leaves my body.
The feeling of happiness, of joy.
It all goes wandering off into the realms around me.
It leaves and sadness overcomes me, it becomes me.
I'm floating, staring down at my body.
I watch as my soul floats away,
observing myself making movements
That I'm supposed to be able to feel.
This happens to me every time.
Each time that I get the news
that someone has passed on.
You've taken your last breath,
seen your last glimpse of human existence.
You're now moving on to whatever it is that's next.
You'll never have to hurt again.
And then I start to think about
how good that must feel
to never have to experience pain again.
I feel nothing, but I also feel everything.
My mind goes blank, my eyes become steady.
I stop blinking. I stop thinking. I stop everything.
I sit there for a while in my emptiness
and know that at some point,
I have to do something, but I want nothing.
I feel nothing. I am nothing.
How am I supposed to find the same joy that I had
just moments before finding out?
How am I supposed to sleep?
To do anything besides sitting here staring into nothing
as tears stream down my face?
This is one of those times when I want
that interaction that I always crave:
The touch of another human.

It reminds me that I am still here.
Lets me know that things will be okay
when I feel like everything has just ended.
This is when I need someone the most,
but no one is anywhere to be found.
It's just me, an empty vessel
trying to hang on to your memory.

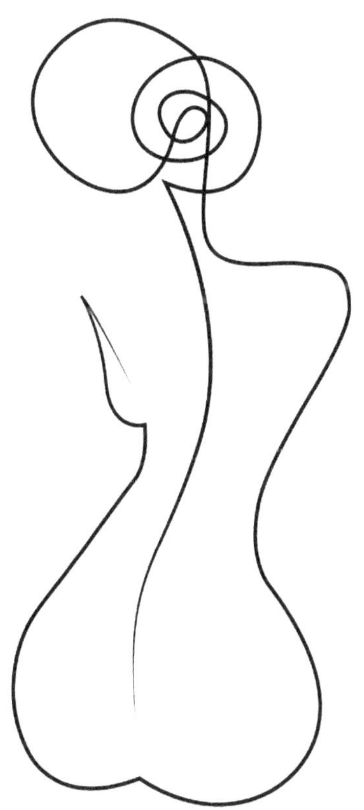

Eyes

These eyes hold more than anyone will ever know
They're looking for comfort
Searching for hope
Peering into the souls of the unknown
They're brave, afraid, and rejecting
Sad, angry, confused
But when you look into these eyes,
You will see no fear.
You will see a girl with strength,
A girl that takes risks,
A girl that puts herself out there
Without much thought.
Your own eyes might be fighting
Trying to uncover the mystery,
But mine?
They don't fight back,
They stand strong
Blocking incoming forces
But why are they blocking?
What's lying behind?
An abyss of darkness
Concealing all the pain
Disguising a tortured soul
A lonely heart
A broken girl
The inside is disastrous,
The outside is beautiful.
These eyes want to move on
They want to find beauty
The beauty they stopped noticing along the way.

Reborn

An idiot a thousand times reborn,
When will I ever learn?
All I do is cause my heart to yearn.

I always tend to wish
For something that I'll never have
I look at them and see a future,
They look back at me and laugh.

They know that they're beginning a game
I think this time it's real,
When it's all over, I'm not the same
My heart is no longer made of steel.

My mind and body start to yearn.
All I do is cause my heart to mourn.
When will I ever learn?
An idiot a thousand times reborn.

A Fragment

A broken shard lain scattered on the ground
Amongst its flock,
A piece too small to make a difference,
A part of something that was once whole
But has now lost its value,
Lost its meaning and aesthetic
Shattered bits of nothingness
Swept up with the dozens of other pieces
And hurdled into the garbage
Validating its now worthless sense of being.

This is how I have felt ever since that night.

I tried to pretend as if it didn't happen
Didn't bother me
Didn't completely demolish my self-worth,
But I've never been able to lie to myself for long.

I'm broken.
Destroyed.
Crumbled.
Completely shredded
Into an infinitesimal speck of existence.

It's hard, if not impossible,
To bring myself back to life.

The life that you stole from me
When you decided to have your way
Without my permission.

Demons

The demons can be really fucking loud sometimes.
They mostly come around when it's silent,
Every single chance that they get
They creep into my mind when things get quiet
And it deafens me.

They become so loud
That I can't focus on anything else
They take over my mind, my entire body
They tell me that I'm not worth anything
That no one loves me
They remind me of all
The horrible things from my past,
They tell me that I'm a horrible person too.

Most times, I can feel them entering my brain,
I completely zone out and my soul leaves my body
I get lost in another realm
And have to fight my way back.
It's sort of like astral projection
Except that I'm awake when it happens
And it happens all the fucking time.
That's the first sign
Of knowing when the demons are near
They distract me in any way that they can
They try to lure my soul away
So they can take my body over.
They want it, but I can't figure out why
Sometimes, I even consider letting them take it.

I've dreamt so much about not being here,
So what if I just give in?
What if I just allow them to have me?
What if I just drift off forever, never to return?

But the thing about letting them win,
Is that I'll never know what it feels like if they do.
I'll never be able to feel anything again.

That used to be all I wanted,
To never feel again.
No more sadness
No more pain
No more disappointment
No more hating myself
But now?
It's lost the appeal.
I've sort of already become numb in several ways,
So what less is there to possibly feel?
The only feelings that matter to me now
Are the ones that I get less often
The feeling of happiness
Of love
Of belonging

If I can't feel anything,
I would never be able to feel those either,
And God do they feel great,
I crave those moments
But the demons always take them away.

They always snatch away
Every bit of joy that I have in my body
They want to leave me with nothing
When that's all I have.

Sometimes the demons can be really fucking loud
That's why I can't stand the silence.

I Came On a Thursday

On what I assume was a chilly afternoon,
At the beginning of November,
When the leaves have all fallen off the trees
The sun shines, but there's still a little chill in the air.

I opened my eyes as I entered a world of unknown.
Unknowing all of the things that I would go through
Unknowing that I had just solidified my place
On this Earth as a human being,
A being that would feel anything but human.
A being that would have to up-stand
So many things that were placed upon her
Before she was even born.

I grew up being told that I had to be this way and that
That I had to go to school
That I had to live up to all of these dreams,
Dreams that my family members couldn't achieve
Because they decided to go down different paths
They married young
They reproduced
They did everything as if
They were living their last days.

In school, I was tormented because of my size
I was told that no man would ever want me
Because I had no thighs
I had no meat on my bones
I was called anorexic
I was called bulimic
I was told that I needed to eat more
I was made to feel that my being
Was less than those around me
Because I looked different
Because I was a skinny little girl that wore glasses
And was afraid to talk to everyone
Because I had so many trust issues

Because of the friendships that had failed
Because of the family
That had turned their backs on me
And treated me as if I was not one of their own.

I got to high school
And then things started to get a little better,
But then I moved and my torment began all over again.
I was told there would be
A new addition to my family
That I would be getting a little brother
I was excited but at the same time,
I felt afraid.
I had spent so many years of my life
Feeling like I wasn't enough
And this made me feel that same way.
Another being would be born into my family
And I knew that he would have
Those same constraints on him as I had
I knew I would have more responsibility as well
Because when he came
A part of me became even more sheltered
Than I had already been.
I had to give up so much of my life,
But I felt that it was worth it because it was him.

When I got to college, I had no idea who I was
Because I was only identified by the things
That people wanted me to be.
While there, I was supposed to find myself
But instead, I found all of these years of misery
I lost my way, but I never really had a way
I had no idea what to do
I started depending on other things
That would keep me out of that feeling,
That would bring me a little more comfort
Because people around me were doing them too.

I Came On a Thursday
And around April 2017, I almost went.
I remember staring off the edge of a balcony,
Thinking I just wanted to jump.
I just wanted all of it to be over with,
But something stopped me,
And about a week later, I tried it again.
I wanted to take all of the pills I saw in the bottle
But something stopped me again.
And after that day, I still had those thoughts
All of those thoughts from my childhood
From when I felt like I wasn't enough.
From when I felt like I wasn't who I should be
Because I had no clue
Who the fuck I was supposed to be in the first place
Because my family never allowed me
To find my own way

I almost went.
But if I had gone, I would not be standing here today
I would not know the things that I know now
I would not have accomplished the things that I have
I would not have found
The one thing that made me happy in this world
I would not have found
The confidence that I ended up gaining
I would not have found
The people that I've loved so much

I almost went.
And I won't lie
Sometimes I think that maybe I should have.
Sometimes I wish that I had done those things
That something wouldn't have stopped me
But in the time that I've still been here
I've realized that I do have someplace in this world
And even though, I still haven't found it
I believe that I hold some type of significance

That I'm here for some bigger reason

So before I go…
I want the world to know that
I fought this demon for my entire life
And it almost won,
It almost conquered,
But I stood my fucking ground
In hopes that one day
My life's meaning would be found.

Woeful Thinking

No one tells you how it really feels to heal
How lonely it is
How many times you'll just want to give up
Give in to the darkness surrounding you
No one walks you through what to do
When you just want a quick fix.

They tell you to go talk to someone
Spend some quality time
But what about those of us that are in it alone?
What do we do?

I have no one to call on.
No one to run to
No shoulder that I can cry on
Because no one understands
No one wants to understand.

They don't want to hear my sob story
They have no desire to listen
To me speak on all the things I've been through
The things I'm fighting with every day
They just want the happy pieces of me,
The pieces that they can take
And use for their own good.

No one wants me when I'm breaking.
They only want me when I'm healed.

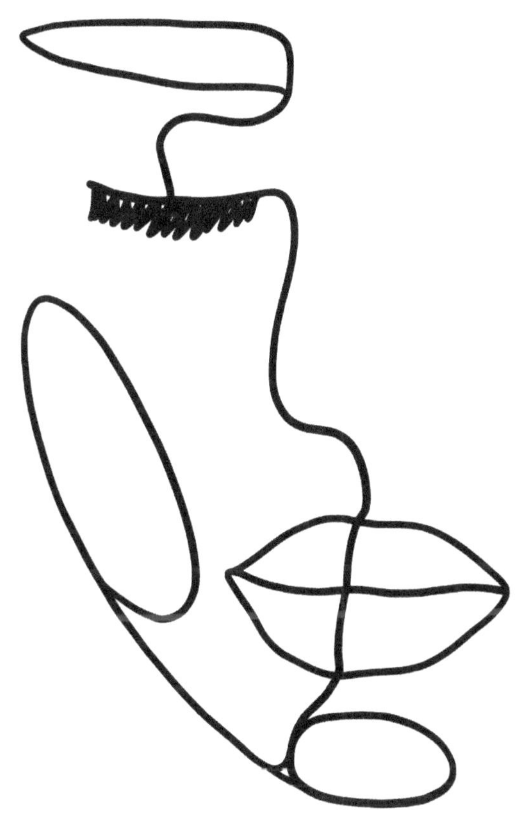

Unwanted

I've always wondered what it feels like to be loved,
To be wanted so badly by someone
That they can't keep me from their thoughts.
To be admired while all my flaws poke out
Like a sore thumb
To be cherished for all of eternity
But the thing about eternity is that it's all an illusion.

There is no forever because everything must end
One day, we will all cease to exist
And the mere mention of my name will hold no weight
Because those that remembered me will be long gone
And even though I know that eternal love
Is not something that I should look forward to,
I still want it.

I desire it as if I were a child
Wandering through a toy store for the very first time,
Seeing so many different options
Wishing that I can have all of them
But knowing that if I'm lucky
I can only have one.
And in all the years of my life
I've still never found that one
Or even felt good enough to be that one.

I'm just a lost child in a toy store
Wandering around looking at all the toys I can't afford
Wishing that some miracle will lend me the perfect one
Not having to endure for it,
Just placing it directly into my hands.

But I'm not a child.
This isn't a toy store.
But I am lost.

A vessel that's been searching for its other half
A half that probably doesn't even exist
In the form of a partner
This half is probably buried deep within my fibers.
Buried under neglect, abuse
Hatred, trauma, and sadness
Lost and wandering around a forest.
Trying desperately to find the burial site
And make myself whole again.

I've always wondered what it feels like to be loved.
Maybe if I'm lucky, I'll find the other half of me,
And cherish her for the rest of eternity.

34

WILD HEART

Lonely & Longing

Loneliness has surrounded me throughout my life,
I've always been alone, which I have no problem with
But the feeling of loneliness is different.
It's like my heart is constantly breaking
My mind endlessly racing
Imagining the comfort of someone else,
Anyone else.
It's a feeling I know all too well
One that has led me to bad decisions
Misleading interactions
Just so that I can escape.
It makes me feel so desperate
Like I'm begging for attention
But I've realized that it's not the attention I want,
It's the interaction.
The physicality
The tangibility
I crave another being around me
I crave someone's touch
But not just anyone's,
Someone who will give me
That feeling I've been missing.
Someone that will make me feel beautiful
Make me long for more of them
When the moment is over.
And that…
That is where you come in.

For You

It's only the beginning,
But it feels like it's close to ending.
I want you, but do I want to?
I like you, but I fear you.
These butterflies won't stop fluttering
My heart won't stop sputtering
Releasing feelings that I wanted to die
But they all come back
When I look into your eyes.

Your eyes. Those eyes
Brown, but filled with so much hope
So much happiness
But what's behind those eyes so bright?
I can only imagine when you hold me tight

Your arms. Those arms
Covered in your favorite form of art
Squeezing me tight enough to touch my heart
But what if I'm thinking too fast?
What if this ends sooner than it lasts?
I don't want to think negatively
But I want you to be mine indefinitely.

Be mine. All mine
So that we can shine
So brightly together
Hoping for forever
But in reality, I know
That we must first take things slow
And yes I know, I know
That some of this happiness will go
But as long as you're mine
Baby, I promise
It will all be just fine

Because when I look into your eyes
Those eyes.
I pray that I never go blind
I would die if I were unable to see your face
See that smile
And even when it's erased
Being around you just makes me feel so great
And I know that somehow
This must be fate
Because before you showed up
I had given up.
My heart had shut down
No longer wanting to drown
In a sea of love with a drastic end
Not wanting to be anything more than friends
But now that you're here
I want to keep you near
And even though I fear
Those eyes
Those arms
That face
That smile,
I'm willing to chase them
For miles and miles
As long as you promise
To treat me right
And hold me tight
For the rest of the night,
For as long as you are in my life.

Retrograde

The tide came rushing in one too many times
But the storm is over now
Only the strong have survived
You kept me in good spirits
When I started to drown
Now you need the same from me
I promise I won't let you down.

Pieces

As I look into your eyes
I see everything that I've ever wanted
All of the pieces of the puzzle
That I could feel myself missing
All of the things I've been yearning for
Wrapped up and sent directly to me
You're what I prayed for
What I always thought I was made for
But the thing about getting what you've always wanted
Is trying to figure out if it's really yours
Or if it's just a trap.
Just a teaser to get you all interested and excited
Only to break your heart once again.
I can see myself feeling things for you
That I have not felt for ages
I can see the way you look at me
And it's not just because
You want to see what's underneath
You want to see what's inside
And show me that side of you.
You want me to feel like
I always have someone to run to
I want to feel the same
But I also want to avoid the pain
How do I have you
And not have to worry about losing you?
In my life, that's what usually happens.
I grow attached to something or someone
Only to have to learn to cope
Without them in the long run.
I want to take this chance
Because I feel like you deserve it.
I just don't want to fuck it up,
And leave myself deserted.

Bliss

Sweet, sweet bliss
The way you took me in those big strong hands
And made me feel like I was oh so small
Like a grain of rice buried in a salt pile
You know it's there, it just doesn't matter
But in your arms
I feel supreme
Like a supernatural force has taken me over
But instead of scaring the shit out of me
I feel your fingers running across my skin
I can feel it in every fiber of my body
You make me feel desired
Like I was the one thing you needed
To survive a horrendous desert heat.
The water your organs so desperately needed
But you're not desperate,
And neither am I.
We're merely two spirits wandering around the universe
Searching for self-actualization,
Self-growth,
And along the paths that we took to get there
We found one another.
The beauty within each other's hearts
The lost entity that desires connection
A connection so deep that it explodes.
A bliss fills my body
Makes my womanhood excited
It sends tingles through my being
Because not only did you have my body,
You had my soul with it.

What if?

It's a question that inhabits my mind
Every time that I think of you.
All the possibilities of
What we did,
What we could,
And probably shouldn't do.

Trust

I have this wall built up
Not wanting to let anyone in
To destroy what's on the other side
My heart.

This wall has come down a couple of times
And the result was permanently damaging.
I tried to patch up the wounds
And slowly put the wall back up
But then you came
And made me question letting it back down.

At first, I refused to do it
But once things seemed to be going well
I considered letting you in.
But I'm struggling to decide
If that's the safest thing for me.

I feel that if I allow myself to trust you,
You may take advantage of it
And do whatever you want
While knowing that I won't suspect anything.

But on the other hand,
What if you don't?
What if you are a good guy that won't hurt me,
But I mess everything up by not trusting you?

It's a hard decision.
One that I don't know if I can make.
Maybe one day I will.
But as of right now,
I remain lost in the middle of the circle of trust.

Garden

I've written about love and sex before
But the emotion you extracted from my body
Was so much more
Your hands caressing me in ways I had missed
My body shaking, longing for your kiss
I never knew a pair of lips could feel so good
I reached ecstasy from your tongue
Exploring my womanhood
Finding its way to that secret spot
The X uncovered a flow more times than not
Your body pressed against mine
Kissing me softly after you'd entered inside
Strokes so deep I could feel them everywhere
Why the fuck did I wait so long to get you here?
My body was flowing
Watering your plant that hadn't stopped growing.

Water

My feelings have bloomed
Like flowers that were carefully tended to
They started simple
But blossomed into something beautiful
Something unique
This is what your conversation has done to me.

You enhanced my mind
You spoke positivity into me
You gave me something to smile about

You watered my soil
My roots began to grow
You shone your light down onto me
And gave me so much hope
You granted me attention that I wasn't used to.

I was dry
Like the sand of the desert
No nurturing
No growth
Just the sweltering sun beaming onto me
Everything surrounding me tried to break me
Longed for me to retreat into the soil
Into the depths of the Earth
I felt myself suffering
I was overcome by dehydration
But then you came along.

You poured your contents onto me
Provided me with your nourishment
You lent me your hand and I grabbed hold
I absorbed you.

My fibers awakened
You were just what I'd been needing
You're the rainfall on a dry day
Watering me at my base
Putting me at ease
You gave me hope to keep growing
To evolve into a beautiful sight
Into a spirit as kind as yours.

A companion
A piece to your puzzle
A calm to your storm
A source of nourishment
So that I can pour my water
Right back into you.

Previous surroundings
Two souls with open minds
Two loners who don't enjoy feeling lonely
Just us,
Alone.
Together.
Finding comfort in each other's presence
In each other's bodies.
You looked at me, over and over
You called me beautiful,
But all that I could see was

The Beauty In You.

The Return

Four years breezed by like the wind on a chilly day
Memories escaped like an exhale taking my breath away
I'm cold, shivering, desperate for some heat
Who knew I'd find it on the day that we remeet
I was met with your embrace
And my body began to thaw
Feelings began to rush out
Like blood from a wound that's raw
You held me in your arms
And it was as if the sun began to shine
My body warmed
And as my anxiety escaped,
I knew I would be just fine.

Craving

Like a smoker who just needs his fix
I just need to be touched

I need to be held
I need to feel desired.

Touch me like it's the last time you'll ever see me
Like you've been longing for me your entire life

Caress my body like it's a work of art
The finest exhibit in a museum

Kiss me like it's the last thing you'll ever do
Like my lips are what you need for survival

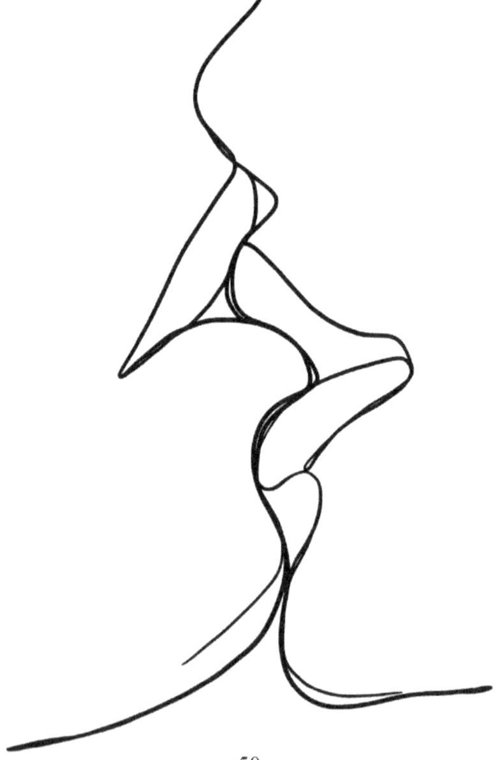

The Road

I don't know where this road will take us
I feel that we have grown apart
Even though we first seemed like a work of art
I didn't want things to be this way
But I don't know what to do
Every moment of my life
Is spent thinking about you.

I don't know where this road will take us
But I hope we don't get lost along the way
I want us to be like we were
Just like yesterday
What happens when we run out of time?
Will you still be here?
Still be mine?

I don't know where this road will take us
But I used to feel that our love was strong
Now I debate on whether or not I should hold on.

Femininity

I'll be honest…
There was someone else
Someone that caught my eye before you did
Someone that had me in the same ways you imagine

I'll be honest…
He took me out for drinks
On one of those nights after I talked to you.
We sat down and after a while,
He expressed his intentions to me
Told me of his hopes
Of one day making me his girlfriend
And eventually his wife.

As I sat there looking at him,
As he spoke to me about love
About vulnerability,
I realized that something had shifted.
Just days before
I had wanted all of these things he was saying to me
But at this moment
I realized that what I really wanted was you.

I had this man in front of me that by textbook
Was what I should be going for
Instead, my heart had been touched by another soul
As he spoke to me
Skepticism clouded the pathway
From my ears to my emotions
Unable to complete the journey
That it takes to get to my heart
And then I thought about you.

About your smile.
Your words.
Your heart.

We connected in less than half the time
That he and I had
And yet your words never
Made me question your intent
We spoke freely from the very beginning
Expressing our admiration and gratitude
For one another.

You awakened the soft side of me
That no one gets to see.
The one that I keep hidden
Because she's been hurt way too many times.

I've always loved love
But it doesn't seem to love me
I always wanted the strong type
The one I've only seen on screen
That Black love
That mad love
That never want you to be sad love
Nothing will ever get in between
What you and I have love
Laying in the bed wide awake
Because I wanna feel your skin
Staring at you while you sleep
Because I'm so grateful that you were created
Crafted with the most beautiful thread
Enclosing a heart that can only be made
From the finest of gold
Making all of my dreams come true
Because little did I know
All of those dreams were about you
So I'll continue to dream until I find you
And hopefully one day I'll awake bound to you

My Forever After

Getaway

A simple setting can feel like another universe
That's the feeling I get when I'm with you
Nothing else in the entire world matters
Just me and you.
You and I.
Enjoying the moment, hoping to have many more
You make me forget all the bad things
I forget how the rest of the world views me
All that matters is who I am to you
The version of me through your eyes
You see parts of me that no one else can
You touch me in ways that no one ever has
You give me solitude
You bring me peace
You give me an image of a serene beach
We're sitting in the sand
Hand in hand
Smoking all our troubles away
You bring me what I've been missing
What I've been needing
You make my mind wander
My body yearns
I miss you when you're away
I think about you when we're apart
What do I do when the person who helps me get away,
Is traveling too close to my heart?

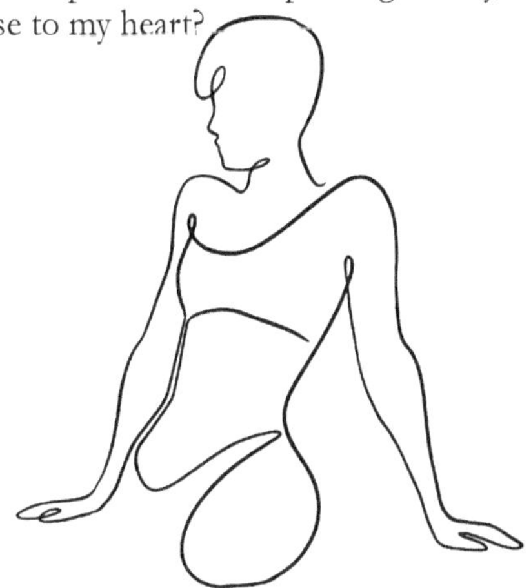

For Me

It's the dick for me.
And I mean that shit respectfully.
I'm constantly thinking about
The things that you do to me sexually,
Physically, emotionally, and mentally
Got me feeling like it was meant to be
Because you see,
No one but you has made my pussy cry tears,
She mourns for you whenever you're not here.
So that's why whenever I get you near,
Her ocean flows so free and so clear.

Waves crashing nonstop
Luring you into your favorite spot
Singing to you like a siren
Got you enticed by her powers as soon as you slide in
Gripping my thighs
Staring into my eyes
Stroke to stroke, you gliding
The passion inside us colliding
Stroking me fast - and then slow.
Seeing how loud you can make me moan
I'm looking back at you and I'm having visions
Like I'm Raven-Symoné
Visions of our time together
And the way that it starts to unfold
I'm catching glimpses
Wondering what it would be like to grow old
Because before you,
It was fuck these men
And I do mean ALL these men.
But now it's FUCK....
I just want this man to be MY man.
Tryna ride with you
Bonnie and Clyde with you
Let the whole world know that I side with you
Like my heart resides with you

It's the dick for me.
And I mean that shit respectfully.
But to be honest,
It's the soul within you that creates this wetness in me.

Smoke In The Air

Your hands are on my thigh
It's never felt so good to be this high
My body turns to mush
I feel myself start to melt
All I can think about is what's underneath your belt
The way you kiss me
The way you graze my skin
I could do this with you again and again
Please don't take it away from me
Let your love stay with me
Let me show you that it's safe with me.

Smoke In The Air

My head is on your chest
Let me help you lay your pain to rest
Let me show you what it's like
For a woman to give her best
Show you that you're nothing like the rest
Let me lift you up
And put that crown back on your head
Appointing you as King
Even when we're not laying in this bed
Let me show you the affection that you deserve
While I listen to you vent every single word
It's something about you that's just so special
I don't even have to imagine your potential
Because it's staring me right in the face
I can feel it every time we embrace.

Smoke In The Air

Our love is in our hands
Let's shake on it
And see how long it stands.

Like a kid in a candy store,
I want it all
Just the thought of you
Turns my emotions raw
I play back what you say to me
Not caring if you mean it
Because baby I go crazy
Every time you get in between it
The way you stroke
I swear I can feel it in my throat
It's the way you look me in my eyes
Bringing your hand up and giving me that gentle choke
You move my legs around in so many ways
I know when this is over, I'll think about it for days
The way you try to fight it when I get on top
Don't tell me you're about to cum
Because to be honest, I might not stop
I know that sounds toxic, but so is that dick
Make me wanna call them other dudes and say
"Aye, it's over with"
This man done snatched my soul
So I'm leaving you out in the cold
This that type of dick that makes me wanna grow old
Every time I get it, it feels like I'm striking gold
And the man that's attached to it
Don't even get me started
Just know that I ain't ever coming back,

Dearly Departed.

Wishful Thinking

I know you're afraid
That's what they forced you to be.
I'm afraid myself
But more for you than me.
We've both been through hell
Trying to love unrequitedly
Mutual feelings of being unseen
Like treasures buried deep within the earth
You see things in me that no one else has
I see the same in you
You wonder why I have these feelings
Why I do the things that I do
There's no simple way to express my reasons
So sit back and relax,
I have a story for you.

I grew up a lonely and confused little girl
I never saw real love
Never thought it would ever exist for me
I never loved myself
No one ever saw great things in me
Those feelings grew deeper
I hated myself
I just wanted someone to accept me
In ways that I couldn't accept myself

I notice the way you look at me
Like you see the beauty within
You care in ways no one ever has
You make me feel beautiful
Like I'm worth more than I ever thought I could be
I tell you things I've never told anyone
And you still cherish me
You're the only person that I can spend days with
And still not want to leave
The only one I want to talk to nonstop.

I know you expect me to be like them,
To use and abuse you
But honestly, I have other plans
None of which involve breaking you
I want to be the woman you deserve
One who will look out for you
Appreciate you,
Love you unconditionally
Do whatever she can to make sure that you're happy.

In return,
I don't want money or material things
Just keep looking at me in the same way
Make my heart skip beats
Make my body long for your touch
Make my mind forget about every man that isn't you

By Night

The sun starts to set
The light begins to fade
All the creations
Become covered in shade

The moon slowly rises
Out come the stars
I look out into the galaxy
Hoping one day it can be ours

I see your face everywhere I turn
My brain finds images
And likes to have them burn

Into my mind
Etched on my heart
But why is it always night
When this image starts?

I believe in the stars
I live by the moon
I light a candle in hope
That I'll see you soon.

With It

Am I crazy?
Maybe baby
But I'm crazy about you
They can flip it
They can twist it
But still, all of this is true
I'm not perfect
You aren't either
But let's just see this through
I'm committed
Are you with it?
We can take things slow
Or we can show the world
Baby we can make it glow
I'll ask you one more time
Because I really need to know
Are you with it?
Really with it?
Because if not
I gotta go.

Lost

In your connection
With no correction
I know that I'm not ready
But that hasn't stopped my thoughts
From moving already
So what do I do?
Why do I think so often about you?
I wonder how this came to be
If this is a sign of something that was meant for me
5 years ago, I first saw your face
5 years later, my mind is constantly running a race
I feel there may be something between us
But each time it has seen us
It doesn't know how to act or what to say
It knows we admire one another
But confused about how to cross the message over
We seem to be very similar
Lost and trying to find direction
Trying to truly find one another
So that we can recover
The bits and pieces of fragments
Left by former lovers
Lost and wanting to grab hold of each other's hand
But not wanting to jump so far
Without knowing how we will land.

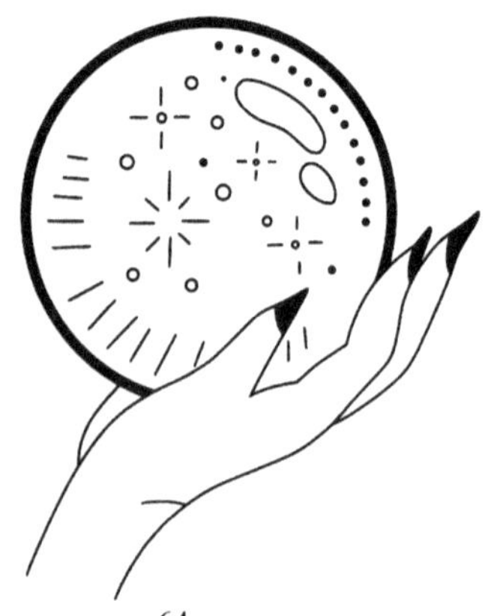

Magnetized

I think I've experienced love at first sight
It was a once-in-a-lifetime sort of thing

I've never forgotten the first day I saw him
The way that he immediately caught my eye

He was magnetic
And I was drawn to him

The attraction was upheld each time I saw him
It became more powerful with each embrace

But I'll also never forget how badly it hurt
When I realized that I wasn't his only magnet

I wasn't special to him at all
I was just his connection for the moment

I think I've experienced love at first sight
And I think it ruined me.

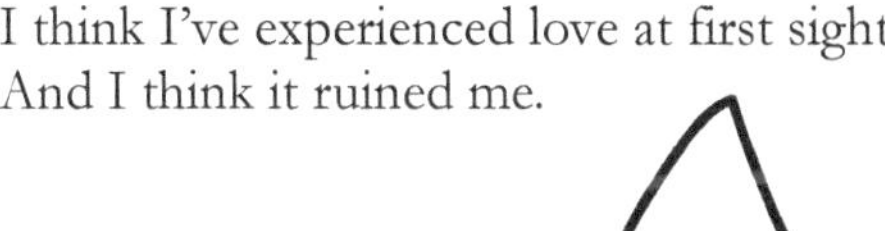

When The Loneliness Starts To Kick In...

All I can do is sit and think
I think about the times we've had
The way you used to make me smile
How much your presence meant to me
I even start to miss you,
But then, I remember.

I remember what you did
I remember why we fell apart
I remember that letting you go was good for me
But will I be able to stop letting people go?
When will I be able to have someone
That won't look to replace me?
When will I be someone's one?
And is that really what I want anymore?
The truth is that I really don't know.

I just hate how lonely it gets
When I'm all alone with no one to talk to
No one to sit around and laugh with
No one to cuddle up to
When all I want is to feel some human contact
It's in these moments
That I start to regret letting you go
But I don't want my loneliness to cause me to settle
I don't want anything unless it's real
Unless it's genuine
I don't want to feel so alone
That I'm willing to run back
To whoever it is that hurt me
I don't want to feel so desperate
That I contact you just to have some interaction
I don't want to feel that I need someone else around.

Unrequited

You said we would be together forever
You said you would never hurt me
But you proved that you are only a liar
I was the best that I could be to you
The best that I had ever been to anyone
But instead of acknowledging that,
You just left me
Hurt, unwanted, and unready to fend for myself
Left my heart torn, and broken
Shattered into a million pieces
Pieces that can never be reconstructed
Left my heart open and bleeding
Bleeding love that could only be replaced by you.

But you don't care,
You never did.
You looked me in the eyes all those times
And said that you loved me
But it was all just a lie
A way to keep me around
To use me for whatever pleasure you desired
Lies to keep me from doing to you
The exact things you were doing to me.

And in the end,
You were the king,
And I the helpless little burden crying
Wanting to be loved
Loved by someone
Anyone better than you;

The love that refused to love back.

Time

Time has passed so briskly
And now that I think about it
Time has always been a thing for us
We wanted more time
Longed for it.
But when the time came
So did those emotions
We had all the time in the world
Which was exactly what we asked for
But the time wasn't what we hoped for.
With time, we grew
Further and further apart
Disdain began to blossom
But unlike how flowers naturally bloom
There was less love running through our veins
The soil became unwatered
Crumbling underneath us
But we didn't seem to notice.

Time.
We had it all and determined that we needed less
Less together
Less arguing
Less irritation
Less of what brought us together in the first place.

Time.
We now needed it apart
It hurt to admit at first
But we've had time
Time to make the best of it all
Time to take advantage
Instead, we let the expiration date creep by
And wondered why we lost
The seemingly everlasting flavor.

We expired
We wilted
We got lost in time.
And now the time has come
To provide us with no more.

71

When Love Becomes Lethal

It washes away everything you once believed in
It changes your heart
It stops your mind from thinking clearly
It takes over your entire body
It sinks into your veins and spreads
Until its venom has reached every crevice
It makes you its prisoner
Forces you to do exactly what it says
It convinces you that what you're doing is right
Everything will be just fine
But then, when you least expect it -
It reaches out and grabs you by the throat
It strangles you
Squeezing until it can find your last breath
And then it releases you.
You think that it is allowing you a second chance
That maybe it cares for you
But then, it attacks again
This time, it aims for your heart
It pulls out its sharpest knife
And stabs you in what seems like the perfect spot
A place where you will be able to feel the most pain
It watches as you collapse
It smiles as you slowly but surely bleed your last drop
This time it shows no mercy
It wipes you out
Leaves you on the ground
Struggling. Confused.
Desperate. Afraid.
Alone.
You lie in agony as it slithers away
Remembering the previous moments
That once felt so precious
You shed a tear,
You speak your last words,
And you wish that you had never been introduced
To such a dangerous drug.

UNBROKEN

Forgiving Myself

I've made some mistakes
I've been through some shit
But I'm still me.

I'm still the same girl who wants to do everything
I still have the same dreams, the same hopes
The mistakes that I've made don't determine who I am
Who I am is determined by what's inside:
A loving soul
A kind spirit
A determined heart constantly seeking love
Searching through passions
This is who I am
This is who I have always been
This is who I will always be, no less
No matter what may lie ahead

I forgive myself for:
hating who I was
wishing for death
harboring hatred
menacing thoughts
waiting too long
moving too slowly
being careless
moving too fast
all the times I lived in the past
giving up
letting myself down
using harsh words
wanting harm
thinking I wasn't enough
letting my health suffer
not putting in enough effort
all I've done
thinking that I was no one.

Now that all is forgiven
It's time to become the girl that I'm meant to be
It's time to gain hope
To lose doubt
Try, even if I struggle, to find a way out
Out of the depths
Out of the sadness
So that my life can be filled with joy and gladness
It's time to love myself for everything I'm worth.

"Cause you're beautiful, like a flower.
More valuable than a diamond.
You are powerful, like a fire.
You can heal the world with your mind and
There is nothing in the world that you cannot do
When you believe in you".
- India Arie

Warrior

The hard times roll in
The darkness starts to sink
I break down
I cry out
I look for comfort
I look for support
I find nothing
The nothing that I hate so much
The nothing that brings something
It brings more hurt
More tears
More disappointment
I can't find a way to shut off the tears
So I resort to my old method
The only thing I know of that works.

I medicate until I can sleep
Sleep the troubles away
Numb the feelings
I dream of better days
Better situations
And when I awake…

I still feel the darkness
But it isn't as deep
I still feel sadness
I still feel hurt
But then I remember…
I remember my past experiences
I remember what I've overcome
I remember who I am
I remember that I can keep going.
Because going is what I do best.

I'm always planning
Always thinking
Always dreaming
But it's time to change my actions
Stop taking each day for granted
Stop wasting time
Start pushing harder
Making every day count
Because I never stay down for long.

No.
Know.
I never stay down for long.

My Apologies

And one day, I swear to God,
I'll pay my mama back
For all the times she taught me
Lessons that I didn't listen.
I think about it every time
I start reminiscing.
But sometimes I just need for her to hear me out,
Really listen to the words coming out of my mouth
Listen to the hurt buried deep within my heart
And after that, maybe my happiness can truly start
Because all I do is sit around
And think about the times
I thought I had it figured out
But much to my surprise
Nothing worked the way
I thought it would way back then
But maybe that's because
I didn't think that I deserved to win
Now I'm still left here wondering
Is this the life that I really wanna be living?
Because I got a picture etched up inside my head
I visualize it every time I wanna wake up dead
But people wanna tell me every which way to go
And I just wanna stop them
Tell them I don't wanna know
Because I don't care about
The money, shoes, cars, and clothes
All I care about is having peace inside my soul
And I hope that when the time comes
God will really know
That I'm sorry for always being so ready to go.

Hatched

I once was a bird
Locked inside a shell
With little room to wiggle
No idea of what was next.
I imagined myself as who I wanted to be,
What I thought would be ideal for me.
I waited and waited
Until the right time to break free
Free from my entrapment
Free from my wandering mind
I crawled out of my shell
Ready to leave the old me behind
I made my way out
Out of my shell of darkness
And into the light.

Standing

Although my heart has been broken
And love has been erased
I have the motivation to move on.
The motivation comes
From knowing that I can live life without you
It gives me a feeling that I wish to keep forever
You see, this feeling
Shows me that I am beautiful.
Beautiful through all the tears
All the lonely nights, heartaches, and bad days
It shows me that I am strong.
Strong enough to piece myself back together
Stand up and show the world that I can't be broken
This feeling gives me faith.
Faith that one day I will love again
And will find the one person
That will make me happy
No matter what it takes.
This is more than just any normal feeling
It is a sign, a symbol.
A representation of me,
Of women,
Of everyone.
To move on and enjoy life
No matter how many times
They have been hurt.
Its a way of saying
"I did it and so can you"
A way of putting a smile
On everyone's face on the worst of days.

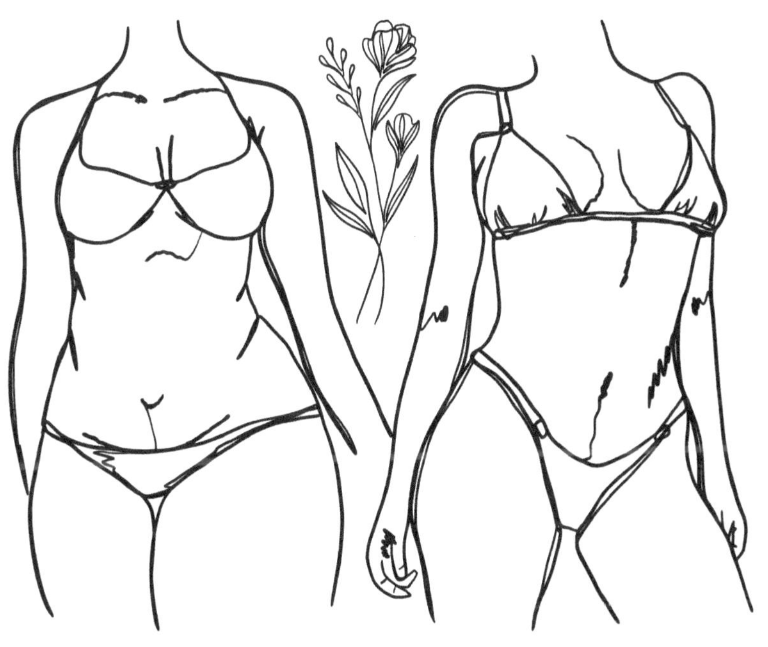

Greatness

I seek and I see greatness within me
Overtaking my being
Freeing me
From the shackles of anxiety.

Feeling free must be freeing.

11:11

The beach has always been where I feel the most alive
The creative aspects of my mind start to thrive
My sickness and my sadness shrivel up and die
The sun basking on my melanated skin
Exhaling and watching my troubles
Fly off into the wind
The breeze in my hair
The sand and waves at my feet
This has to be the closest thing to harmony.

Vision

Stepping into the light
My body struggles to function
I've been surrounded by darkness my entire life.
My vision starts to clear
I can see things that weren't there before.
I've been given a brand new set of eyes,
A different lens.
I should feel happy about this
And don't get me wrong
I am.
But I remember what I'm leaving behind.

What if this newfound vision slips away,
The same way it does when we grow old?
Will I have to go back to the dark place?
That cave that I had become so familiar with?
I'm afraid to go back
Petrified.

So let's play things differently this time.
I'll walk back towards the cave, but not to enter,
To lock the door forever.
Behind that door will lie all of my dark thoughts
The suicidal ideations
The torment
The hatred.
I'll lock it all up and throw the key
In a place where I'll never find it again.

I've finally realized that I have control
I'm the gatekeeper
I decide who enters, and who exits
So behind that door
I'll also lock away the ones that have hurt me
The men that broke my heart
The people that used me
The family that outcasted me

The friends that betrayed me
I'll lock them all together
So they can have the time of their life
Sharing stories about how they almost broke me.

And outside of that door,
I'll be living freely
Loving who I am and the opportunities ahead of me
I'll shed my skin
Shift into a better life
Glide away with my new vision
In a brand new light.

ABOUT THE AUTHOR

Danyelle Latrese is an entrepreneur, creator, former model, and mental health advocate that has always dreamed of being an author. She began writing poetry at the age of 15 as a way to express herself while battling mental health.

Seeking Harmony is a collection of her writing over the years and her first published work

@danyellelatrese
danyellelatrese.com